# The Beaver Dam Railroad

# and the

# Crandull & Shady Valley Railway

# of

# Johnson County, Tennessee

**The Beaver Dam Railroad and the Crandull & Shady Valley Railway of Johnson County, Tennessee**



First Edition

**ISBN: 978-1-387-55991-6**

Non-Fiction books by Doug McGuinn:

*The "Virginia Creeper": Remembering the Virginia-Carolina Railway*

*Green Gold: The Story of the Hassinger Lumber Company of Konnarock, Virginia*

*The Last Train from Elkland*

*The "Railroad to Nowhere": The Deep Gap Tie & Lumber Company Railroad and other Northwestern North Carolina Business Ventures*

*The "Lopsided Three": A History of Railroading, Logging and Mining in the Holston, Doe and Watauga Valleys of Northeast Tennessee*

*The Laurel Fork Railway of Carter County, Tennessee*

*The Beaver Dam Railroad and the Crandull & Shady Valley Railway of Johnson County, Tennessee*

*There's Copper in Them Thar Hills!: Copper Mining in Watauga, Ashe and Alleghany Counties of North Carolina*

To purchase these books, visit

*https://www.lulu.com/search?page=1&q=Doug+McGuinn&adult_audience_rating=00*

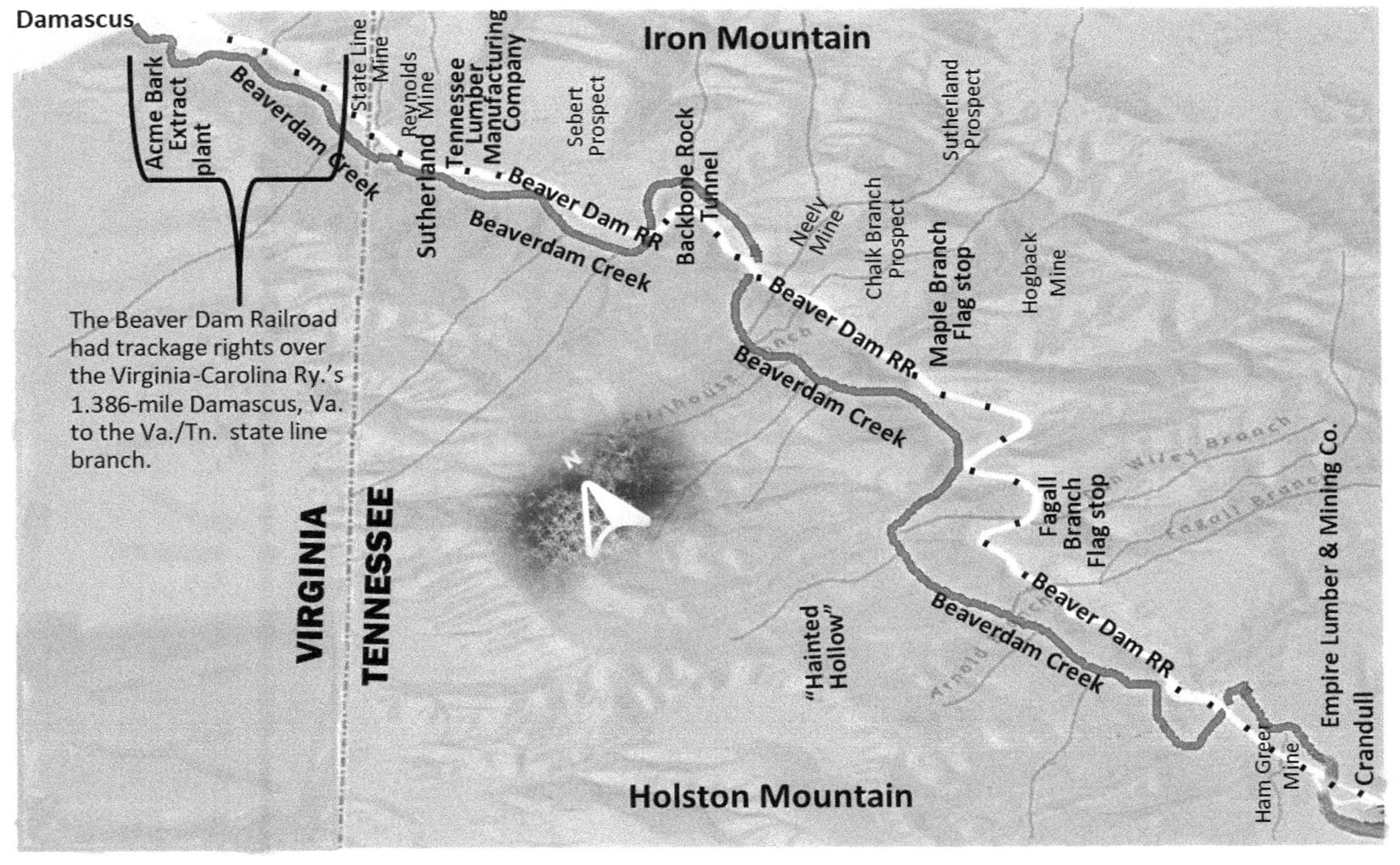
Damascus
Iron Mountain
Acme Bark Extract plant
Beaverdam Creek
State Line Mine
Reynolds Mine
Sutherland
Tennessee Lumber Manufacturing Company
Sebert Prospect
Beaver Dam RR
Beaverdam Creek
Backbone Rock Tunnel
Neely Mine
Chalk Branch Prospect
Sutherland Prospect
Maple Branch Flag stop
Hogback Mine
Beaver Dam RR
Beaverdam Creek
The Beaver Dam Railroad had trackage rights over the Virginia-Carolina Ry.'s 1.386-mile Damascus, Va. to the Va./Tn. state line branch.
VIRGINIA
TENNESSEE
N
"Hainted Hollow"
Fagall Branch Flag stop
Beaver Dam RR
Beaverdam Creek
Empire Lumber & Mining Co.
Ham Greer Mine
Crandull
Holston Mountain

# INTRODUCTION

Shady Valley

*Empire Lumber & Mining Company. – Robert Gray, C.E., Bristol, Va Tenn., advises us that the road which this company proposes to build will be 18 miles long, running from the Holston River to Shady Valley, Tenn. The surveys have been completed and contracts are to be let at once. A. J. Dull, Harrisburg, Pa., is president, G. F. Craig treasurer, and George Warney secretary. Headquarters, Drexel building, Philadelphia, Pa.*

—From *The Railway Age* (vol. 28, July 1 – December 31, 1899)

Shady Valley, located in the northwestern part of northeastern Tennessee's Johnson County, was an isolated cove surrounded by the Holston and Iron mountains with drainage down Beaverdam Creek to Damascus, Virginia. In the flat upper area, was a stand of white pine, said to be unequaled anywhere.

That isolation, however, ended during the late 1890s, when the George Craig & Sons Lumber Company of Winterburn, West Virginia, "discovered" Shady Valley. The Craig family formed the Empire Lumber and Mining Company to exploit the timber and manganese deposits in upper Shady Valley.

Because there was no railroad to Shady Valley, the company built an 18-mile-long wagon road from south of Abingdon, Virginia, across Holston Mountain and into Shady Valley. The company hauled boilers and parts for its double-cut (it sawed both coming and going) band mill across the mountain from Bristol, Virginia/Tennessee.

Benjamin H. Adams, Sr., who worked for both the Empire Lumber & Mining Company and the Tennessee Lumber Manufacturing Company (the Tennessee Lumber Manufacturing Company, also located in Shady Valley, will be discussed later in this book), describes his experience:

> *I was about eleven years old when I got my first paying job. The Empire Lumber Company was bringing boilers from Bristol, Virginia. These boilers were needed for the planing mill. They had to be taken through Denton's Valley and across Holston Mountain. Oxen were used to pull the boilers up the mountain; mules, steel cable, and block-and-tackle dropped the boilers down the mountain. I was the water boy. The men made a yoke and placed it across my shoulders, and I could carry two buckets at once. Before the job was finished, I was supplying water over a seven-mile stretch.*

In 1900, the Empire Lumber and Mining Company located a site for its mill, 8.5 miles south of the Virginia/Tennessee state line, in Johnson County, Tennessee, at a community now called Crandull[3], assembled their sawmill and began sawing, even though there was no railroad for them to ship the finished lumber.

The Virginia–Carolina Railway's track, originating at Abingdon, was completed to Damascus, 16 miles away, on February 7, 1900, and, shortly thereafter, the V–CRy opened a 1.84-mile branch from Damascus to the Va./Tn. state line, mainly to be able to take the area mills' tan bark to the Acme Bark Extract plant (later, the site of the Smethport Extract Company's plant)[4], about four-tenths of a mile south of Damascus.

Wilton E. Mingea, President Virginia–Carolina Railway

The Empire Lumber and Mining Company wanted to be able to use the V–CRy's branch line. That way, not only could they take their tan bark to the Acme Bark Extract plant they could also take their cars of lumber to Damascus, where they would be pulled to Abingdon via the V–CRy's mainline and left in the Abingdon yard, waiting to be shipped to out-of-state markets by Norfolk & Western or some other major railroad. Another reason the Empire Lumber and Mining Company wanted access to V–CRy's branch line was to be able to turn its engines on the turntable located in nearby Laureldale, so they wouldn't have to return to the mill in reverse! First of all, though, a railroad would have to be built from their mill to the state line.

The Craig family loaned the funds to build a railroad to its mill, and as a result, the Beaver Dam Railroad was chartered on August 6, 1900, under the laws of Tennessee, George F. Craig the president and general manager of the railroad; Jas. Faulkner, Jr., the assistant general manager.

George F. Craig, his wife and two of their children, Winterburn, WV

# "THE SHORTEST RAILROAD TUNNEL IN THE WORLD"

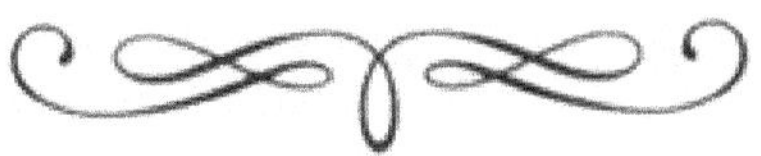

Backbone Rock Tunnel, c. 1910

When the first train reached Damascus on the 7th day of February 1900, the building of the Beaver Dam Railroad from the Va./Tn. state line to the Empire Lumber and Mining Company's mill was rapidly pushed. Wilton Mingea, the president of the Virginia–Carolina Railway, had already agreed to grant the Beaver Dam Railroad trackage rights over the V–CRy's branch[5] from Damascus to the Va./Tn. state line for an annual rent of $300.

In 1901, while the Empire Lumber and Mining Company was laying track for the Beaver Dam Railroad to connect with the Virginia–Carolina Railway's branch line, they came to a stone ridge that stood seventy-five feet high and was approximately twenty-six feet thick. The ridge was named Backbone Rock because of its appearance. This rock, which was above the Sutherland community, is an extension of the Iron Mountain range. Beaverdam Creek flows around the end of the rock.

Crew Foreman E. A. Foster, who had come from Richmond, Virginia, to supervise the building of the Beaver Dam Railroad, had to decide whether to follow Beaverdam Creek around the end of the rock or to blast a short tunnel through the rock to lay the BDRR's track. Foster chose the latter.

Tunneling through Backbone Rock

The Beaver Dam Railroad was opened for traffic on May 13, 1901, and a sizable business developed in logging, lumbering, and the movement of manganese ore.

The first train to run, however, immediately encountered a problem: the smokestack of the train's engine couldn't pass through the tunnel. The top of the tunnel had to be hand-chiseled to eliminate this problem. At a mere twenty feet in length, the Backbone Rock Tunnel quickly became known as "The shortest railroad tunnel in the world."

Celebrating the completion of the Backbone Rock Tunnel

Panoramic view of Backbone Rock
and the Backbone Rock Tunnel

# THE EMPIRE LUMBER AND MINING COMPANY AND THE TENNESSEE LUMBER MANUFACTURING COMPANY

The Empire Lumber and Mining Co.'s train
on the Beaver Dam Railroad's track

*The Empire Lumber and Mining Company, of Bristol, Tenn., will operate a brick plant in Shady Valley, Johnson County, in order to manufacture all the brick required in the construction of a large lumber plant in the valley.*

—From *The Clay-Worker* (vols. 33-34, 1900)

**Empire Lumber and Mining Company, Crandull, Tenn.**

By the time their railroad arrived, on May 13, 1901, the Empire Lumber and Mining Company's mill had over one million board feet of lumber ready to ship out.

Lumber yard, Empire Lumber and Mining Company

Loggers, Empire Lumber and Mining Company

*The Tennessee Lumber Manufacturing Company, now building a lumber plant at Sutherland, Johnson County, has increased its capital stock from $60,000 to $120,000. The new plant will soon be put in operation. It will have a daily capacity of 80,000 feet.*

*—From The Lumber Trade Journal* (Nov. 1, 1901)

Another Shady Valley lumber company that grew with the presence of the Beaver Dam Railroad was the Tennessee Lumber Manufacturing Company, which in 1900 built a camp about three miles south of Damascus, in the Sutherland, Tennessee, community, and set

**Tennessee Lumber Manufacturing Company, Sutherland, Tenn.**

up a mill to cut timber. The company hired 400 men to keep the operation running. The Tennessee Lumber Manufacturing Company sawed 80,000 board feet a day.

The Tennessee Lumber Manufacturing Company created its own company town, building houses for the loggers and their families. A large commissary, which supplied groceries, hardware, grain for animals, and some clothing and yard goods, was also built. The post office was also in this building. In addition, there were company offices, a railroad station, a boarding house, and a doctor's office. And, as soon as possible, a combination church and school building was erected.

**Tennessee Lumber Manufacturing Company, Sutherland, Tenn.**

# ROLLING STOCK

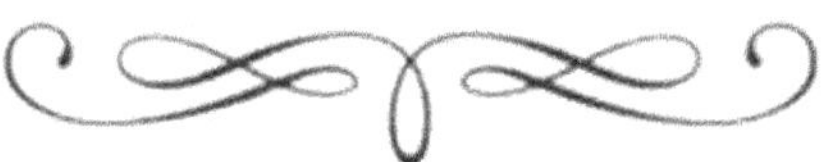

# VIRGINIA-CAROLINA RAILWAY CO.

## BEAVER DAM RAILROAD CO.

**W. E. MINGEA**, President, Gen. Mgr. and Treas. Va. Car. Ry., Abingdon, Va.
**GEO. F. CRAIG**, Prest. and Gen. Mgr. Beaver Dam R.R., Philadelphia, Pa.
**GEO. F. CRAIG**, Vice-President Va.-Car. Ry., 726 Drexel Building, "
**P. G. WRIGHT**, Supt. Virginia-Carolina Ry., Abingdon, Va.
**J. W. BELL**, Secretary Virginia-Carolina Ry., "
**L. F. CROSBY**, Cashier and Auditor, Va.-Car. Ry., "

| 3 | 1 | Mls | *December 8, 1904.* | 2 | 4 |
|---|---|---|---|---|---|
| Noon | A M | | LEAVE] [ARRIVE | A M | P M |
| †12 01 | †7 20 | 0 | □ ....... **Abingdon**[1] ....... ♁ | 11 30 | 5 30 |
| 12 23 | 7 40 | 4.4 | ....... Watauga ....... | 11 00 | 5 02 |
| 12 45 | 8 00 | 9.2 | ....... Barron ....... ♁ | 10 40 | 4 40 |
| 1 00 | 8 14 | 13.0 | ....... Drowning Ford ....... | 10 15 | 4 23 |
| 1 09 | 8 22 | 14.5 | ....... Mock's Mill ....... | 10 06 | 4 16 |
| 1 15 | 8 27 | 16.0 | arr.. **West Damascus** ♁ lve. | 10 00 | 4 10 |
| 3 23 | 9 24 | 16.5 | lve.. **West Damascus** ..arr. | 9 50 | 4 01 |
| 3 34 | 9 35 | 17.8 | arr.... State Line .... lve. | †9 39 | †3 50 |
| | | | *(Beaver Dam R.R.)* | | |
| †3 50 | †9 40 | 17.8 | lve..... State Line .... arr. | 9 35 | 3 30 |
| 3 55 | 9 45 | 18.8 | ....... Sutherland ....... ♁ | 9 30 | 3 26 |
| 4 19 | 10 10 | 23.0 | ....... Fagall ....... | 9 05 | 3 02 |
| 4 35 | 10 25 | 25.7 | ....... **Crandull** ....... ♁ | †8 50 | †2 45 |
| P M | A M | | ARRIVE] [LEAVE | A M | P M |

□ Norfolk & Western Ry. station.

† Daily, except Sunday.
STANDARD—*Eastern time.*
**Connection.**—[1] At Abingdon—With Norfolk & Western Ry.

Records of locomotive and car ownership of the Beaver Dam Railroad Company are sparse. What is known is that the Empire Lumber and Mining Company, owner of the Beaver Dam Railroad, paid the Virginia–Carolina Railway Company $300 per month to lease from June 30, 1902 to June 30, 1905 an engine[6], a combination car[7], and crew.

V–CRy's Engine #1 (leased to BDRR) at Bridge #1

The various lumber and mining companies adjacent to the railroad used their own locomotives while operating over the Beaver Dam Railroad track. For instance, the Empire Lumber and Mining Company had its own 0-4-0T engine[8] and the Tennessee Lumber Manufacturing Company had its own 50-ton, 2-truck Shay locomotive[9].

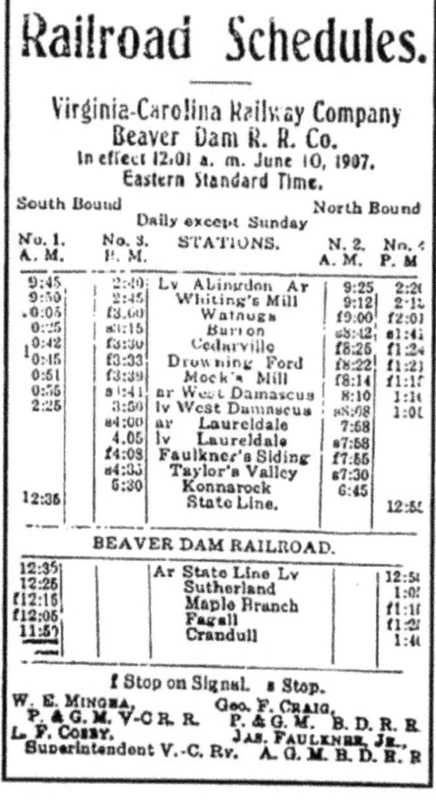

# Railroad Schedules.

Virginia-Carolina Railway Company
Beaver Dam R. R. Co.
In effect 12:01 a. m. June 10, 1907.
Eastern Standard Time.

South Bound — Daily except Sunday — North Bound

| No. 1. A. M. | No. 3. P. M. | STATIONS. | N. 2. A. M. | No. 4 P. M |
|---|---|---|---|---|
| 9:45 | 2:40 | Lv Abingdon Ar | 9:25 | 2:2 |
| 9:50 | 2:45 | Whiting's Mill | 9:12 | 2:1 |
| .0:05 | f3.00 | Watauga | f9:00 | f2:01 |
| 0:25 | s3:15 | Barron | s8:42 | s1:4 |
| 0:42 | f3:30 | Cedarville | f8:25 | f1:2 |
| 0:45 | f3:33 | Drowning Ford | f8:22 | f1:21 |
| 0:51 | f3:39 | Mock's Mill | f8:14 | f1:1 |
| 0:55 | s3:41 | ar West Damascus | 8:10 | 1:1 |
| 2:25 | 3:50 | lv West Damascus | s8:08 | 1:0 |
| | s4:00 | ar Laureldale | 7:58 | |
| | 4.05 | lv Laureldale | s7:58 | |
| | f4:08 | Faulkner's Siding | f7:55 | |
| | s4:33 | Taylor's Valley | s7:30 | |
| | 5:30 | Konnarock | 6:45 | |
| 12:35 | | State Line. | | 12:5 |

BEAVER DAM RAILROAD.

| | | | | |
|---|---|---|---|---|
| 12:35 | | Ar State Line Lv | | 12:5 |
| 12:25 | | Sutherland | | 1:0 |
| f12:15 | | Maple Branch | | f1:1 |
| f12:05 | | Fagall | | f1:2 |
| 11:57 | | Crandull | | 1:4 |

f Stop on Signal. s Stop.

W. E. Mingea, P. & G. M. V-C R. R.
Geo. F. Craig, P. & G. M. B. D. R. R
L. F. Cosby, Superintendent V.-C. Ry.
Jas. Faulkner, Jr., A. G. M. B. D. R. R

Although primarily a logging line, the Beaver Dam Railroad also provided passenger service from the Virginia–Carolina Railway's then end-of-line near Taylor's Valley in Virginia to the Tennessee state line and beyond, terminating at Crandull, Tenn., with a regular stop along the way at Sutherland, Tenn. and flag stops[10] at Maple Branch and Fagall Branch.

The Beaver Dam Railroad's train ran six days per week (every day except Sundays), making one round trip a day from the Virginia side of the Va./Tn. state line to Crandull.

# THE SHADY VALLEY MINES

Loading platform of a Shady Valley mine

Because the Shady Valley soil is almost a dark-red – the result of manganese dioxide – many manganese-ore mines and prospects were located near the right-of-way of the Beaver Dam Railroad. Not only did the BDRR do a sizeable business hauling logs, its cars also hauled this ore.

Johnson County, Tennessee, consists of three mining districts[11] – Mountain City, Shady Valley, and Butler – the first two lying completely in the county, about 90% of the Butler District lying in Johnson County and about 10% in Carter County. The Shady Valley District lies in the northwestern part of Johnson County. The Shady Valley mines were served by the Beaver Dam Railroad.

**Johnson County, Tennessee, Mining Districts**

Below is a partial list of the mines and prospects (north to south) either beside or near the Beaver Dam Railroad's right-of-way:

| Name | Location |
|---|---|
| 1. Reynolds Mine | Elliot Branch, Iron Mtn. |
| 2. Neely Mine | Owens Branch, Iron Mtn. |
| 3. Sutherland Pros. | Seng Cove Branch, Iron Mtn. |
| 4. Hogback Mine | Cave Spring Branch, Iron Mtn. |
| 5. Davis Mine | McQueen Branch, Holston Mtn. |

(G. W. Stone and F. C. Shrader visited these and other east Tennessee mines and prospects between April and October 1918 and published their findings in an October 1918 report titled *Manganese Deposits of East Tennessee*. Stone and Shrader's findings of the Shady Valley mines listed above are presented below. [Text in brackets and all superscripts are by Doug McGuinn]):

**Reynolds Mine**

*The Reynolds Mine is 1.5 miles south from Damascus, Va., and just south of the Virginia State line, and three-fourths mile northeast of Sutherland. The property is owned by A. D. Reynolds of Bristol. The Lehigh Manganese Company of Bethlehem, Pa., and Damascus, Va., have leased the property and began development in June 1918. By October 100 tons of ore had been mined, about half of which have been shipped. It is reported to average 40% manganese, 13% silica.*

*The mine is on a terraced spur on the northwest slope of Iron Mountain, at an elevation of 2,400 feet, or 450 feet above the creek* [Beaverdam Creek]. *It is in red and yellow clay. The deposit is opened by several cuts not over 10 feet deep and covering a vertical range of 50 feet on the slope. Most of the ore is scattered in the clay. A bed of soft ore about a foot in thickness was observed near the north end of the property.*

*The ore is sledded down the steep slope to the washer*[12] *230 feet below the mine and the washed ore is hauled in wagons to the railroad.*

## Neely Mine

*The Neely Mine is one mile south of Sutherland on the east side of Beaverdam Creek, on the Government Forest Reserve* [now a part of the Cherokee National Forest]. *The manganese deposit was first opened by J. A. Neely, of Damascus. It is now being operated by the Laurel Mining Company, of Mountain City, [Tennessee], in which the Southern Manganese Corporation holds one-third interest. It was worked about 1898 for iron ore. Twenty-seven tons of manganese ore, mostly from the old dumps, has recently been shipped and about four tons lie on the dump. The ore is dry-screened*[13] *and is reported to run about 45% manganese, 4% silica when washed. A road from the mine to the railroad is to be built and a washer installed. The ore is at present hauled to the railroad on sleds.*

*The prospect is on a bench on the northwest slope of Iron Mountain, at 2,800 feet in elevation, 600 feet above the creek. It is in reddish-brown clay. The main opening is a 50-foot cut running northeast into the ridge, following an ore zone* *about 8 feet thick which dips about $20^0$ NNW. The pit is 20 feet wide and 15 feet high at the face. The ore shipped came from this pit, which is the original working reopened.*

*About 250 feet northeast of the main pit another old working is being reopened and shows considerable scattered ore. It has been reported since the visit by the writer that a solid body of ore has been struck in this working. The prospects are bright for an active mine at this place.*

## Sutherland Prospect

*The Sutherland prospect is 1.75 miles southwest of Sutherland on lands of the U.S. Forest Reserve* [a part of today's Cherokee National Forest]*, which has recently been prospected under lease from the Government by Wiley and J. F. Sutherland, and the indications are reported to be exceptionally favorable. Geologic conditions are believed to be the same as the Neely mine.*

## Hogback Mine

*The Hogback Mine is 2.5 miles south-southwest of Sutherland, on the Government Forest Reserve* [a part of today's Cherokee National Forest]. *It was first opened in 1888 by David Blevins, of Shady Valley, for William McGovern, of Pennsylvania. It has only recently been developed and is now operated by the Lehigh*

*Valley Manganese Company, of Bethlehem, Pa., with an office at Damascus, Va. Operations began early in 1918, and by October they had mined and shipped about 80 tons and had a like amount at the mine ready to ship. It is reported to run 42% manganese, 8% iron, 12% silica. It is at present dry-screened and hand-picked, and in part washed by hose in loading the cars by gravity, but a washer is to be constructed.*

*The mine is on a bench on the northwest slope of Iron Mountain, at an elevation of 2,900 feet, 650 feet above the creek* [Beaverdam Creek]. *The deposit is in brownish and red clay. It is opened by several cuts about 10 feet deep with a vertical range of 100 feet, all showing ore. The best exposure is in a cut 60 feet long. The indications are regarded as favorable for successful mining.*

## Davis Mine

*The Davis mine, called also Parker, or Crandull, mine, is just west of Crandull at the lower end of Shady Valley. The openings are on a flat-topped spur on the west side of the valley 100 to 200 feet above the present valley bottom, adjacent to the site of the old Heberlin mine, from which 800 tons of manganese are reported to have been taken years ago. Since the time of the visit of the writer, October 1917, the mine has been leased to the Southern Manganese Corporation and is at present being operated by them.*

*The property was developed by George E. Davis, of Bristol, Va., who opened several pits and shipped a carload of ore, which is reported to have run about 43% manganese. The lower openings, on the outer edge of the terrace about 100 feet above the valley bottom, are on E. N. Martin's land and are shallow pits in yellow clay and dark manganiferous clay, showing considerable high-grade crystalline manganese ore, probably manganite, and some iron ore. The face of one small pit was almost solid ore, and almost considerable ore is iron, the quantity of high-grade manganese ore from the pit looked very promising.*

*In June, 1918, this property was leased to the Southern Manganese Corporation, which is equipping it with machinery and will begin active operation at once. The tract includes the pits of the old Heberlin mine, whose waste dump contains sufficient nodules of psilomelane to be reworked and profitably washed. Analysis of a carload of the better grade ore shipped during 1917 ran 45.18% manganese, 9.77% iron, and caprock, also shipped in 1917, ran 20.17% manganese, 27.10% iron, and 13.94% silica.*

*The mine has recently (October, 1918) been visited by Mr. Schrader, who reports marked activity. Lodging and commissary buildings to accommodate 80 men are nearing completion. The washer and pumping plants have been erected and electric lights are being installed so that the washer can be run day and night in two shifts. The present production of 16 tons of washed ore a day is planned to increase to 40 tons. The dirt is removed by mule plows and scrapers, dumped through a trap door to tram cars and conveyed by gravity over a double track trestle, to the 25-foot double-log washer 60 feet from the lower end of the mine, where it is dumped by the tilting of the car. The washed ore is hauled by wagon to the railroad at Crandull. The pumping plant is at Crandull, on Beaverdam Creek, and has a capacity of 300 gallons a minute.*

*The ore shipped is reported to run 41% manganese, 10% iron, and 8% silica. The development work has been well planned by the company's engineers, and if the deposit proves as large as is hoped, the use of a steam shovel and other enlargements of the plant will also be made.*

(The two largest operations in the Shady Valley Mining District were the Davis Mine and the Ham [Hamilton] Greer Mine.)

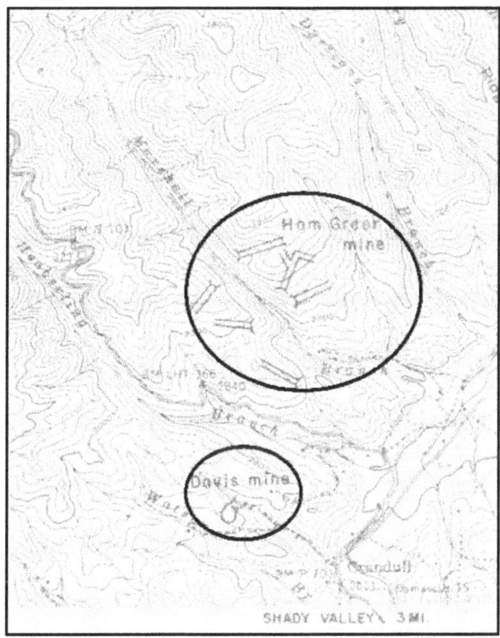

The Davis Mine, which was located ¼ mile west-northwest of Crandull, at the lower end of Shady Valley, was opened for iron ore mining before World War I (the exact date is unknown), reopened in 1917 by G. E. Davis of Bristol, Va./Tn., taken over in 1918 by the Southern Manganese Corporation of Birmingham, Alabama, stood idle from 1919 until 1932, reopened again in 1933, this time by the Tennessee Manganese Corporation, subleased in 1936 to R. U. Butler, and permanently closed in 1938.

Between 1917 and 1938, the Davis Mine produced 1,400 tons of manganese concentrate. In 1917 and 1918, the "wash ore" was removed from the pit by mule plows and scrapers, dumped through a trap hopper into tram-cars, and conveyed by gravity over a double-track trestle to the 25-foot, double-log washer, 60 feet from the lower end of the mine. The washed ore was hauled by wagon to the railroad at Crandull. R. U. Butler, who subleased the mine from 1936 until 1938, however, mined hydraulically by use of water pumped from Beaverdam Creek at Crandull. The ore was washed from a large open pit. The double-log washer product was passed through a single-log washer, if additional washing was needed.

The Ham Greer Mine was located about 3,000 feet north of the Davis Mine. Situated on both sides of Marshall Branch (a tributary of Beaverdam Creek), the Ham Greer Mine was opened in 1938 and closed in late 1942. During this time, approximately 2,627 tons of manganese ore were mined.

Ham Greer Mine

In 1905, an effort was made by the Empire Lumber and Mining Company to develop a tract of ore near the southern end of Shady Valley. A modern washer was erected, and work was carried on for about two years. But in all this time, only about six carloads of ore[14] were shipped. By 1912, the washer had been completely dismantled.

During the late 1940s, the Shady Valley mines (what few were still operating) received a brief renewed lease on life when the U.S. government started to stockpile manganese. Because by then the Beaver Dam Railroad had been abandoned (the abandonment will be discussed later in this book), the ore had to be trucked to Damascus and shipped out of there by rail on the Abingdon Branch of Norfolk & Western Railway (the former Virginia–Carolina Railway).

# THE

# CRANDULL & SHADY VALLEY

# RAILWAY

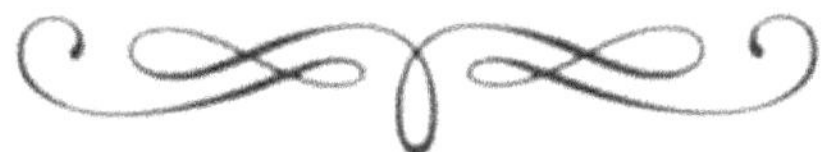

## BEAVER DAM RAILROAD COMPANY.

## CRANDULL & SHADY VALLEY RAILWAY COMPANY.

C. A. BACKER, President, 53 State St., Boston, Mass.

J. E. ROONEY, General Manager, Damascus, Va.

Z. U. WEISZ, Secretary, 53 State St., Boston, Mass.

H. M. COX, Treasurer and Auditor, Damascus, Va.

General Offices—Damascus, Va.

| No. 3 | No 1 | Mls | *April* 18, 1910. | No. 2 | No. 4 |
|---|---|---|---|---|---|
| | | | LEAVE / ARRIVE | | |
| †4 20 P M | †10 30 A M | 0 | Damascus[1], Va | 3 45 P M | |
| — — | — — | 1 | Extract Plant, Va. | — — | 4 50 P M |
| 4 35 P M | 10 45 » | 3 | arr... Sutherland, Tenn ..lve. | 3 50 » | †4 40 P M |
| | 10 45 » | 3 | lve... Sutherland, Tenn ..arr. | 3 30 » | |
| | 11 05 » | 7 | Fagall, Tenn | 3 02 » | |
| | 11 25 » | 10 | arr ... Crandull, Tenn ... lve. | 2 50 » | |
| | 11 25 » | 10 | lve.... Crandull, Tenn ...arr. | 2 15 » | |
| | 11 45 » | 14 | Bristol Road, Tenn | 2 00 » | |
| | 11 55 A M | 16 | Shady, Tenn | †1 50 P M | |
| | | | ARRIVE / LEAVE | | |

Trains marked † run daily, except Sunday.

STANDARD—*Eastern time.*

**Connections**—[1] With Virginia-Carolina Ry. and Laurel Ry.

*The Crandull & Shady Valley Railway Company of Johnson County, Tennessee, has been charted by the state with $10,000 capital. The incorporators are R. E. Butler and W. T. Smythe. The company proposes to construct a railroad from Crandull, Johnson County, up Beaverdam Creek to a point on top of Cross Mountain, in Johnson County.*

—From *Engineering and Contracting* (vol. 32, 1909)

A separate entity, the Crandull & Shady Valley Railway, was chartered on December 15, 1909, under the laws of Tennessee, and built a six-mile extension of the Beaver Dam Railroad, from Crandull to the community of Shady. Beyond Shady, approximately two additional miles of tracks serving the lower Shady Valley ore developments were constructed.

(The map on the next page shows, inside oval, the approximate area served by the C&SVRy.)

Although the two railroads (the Beaver Dam Railroad and the Crandull & Shady Valley Railway) had separate corporate structures, they always operated as a single unit.

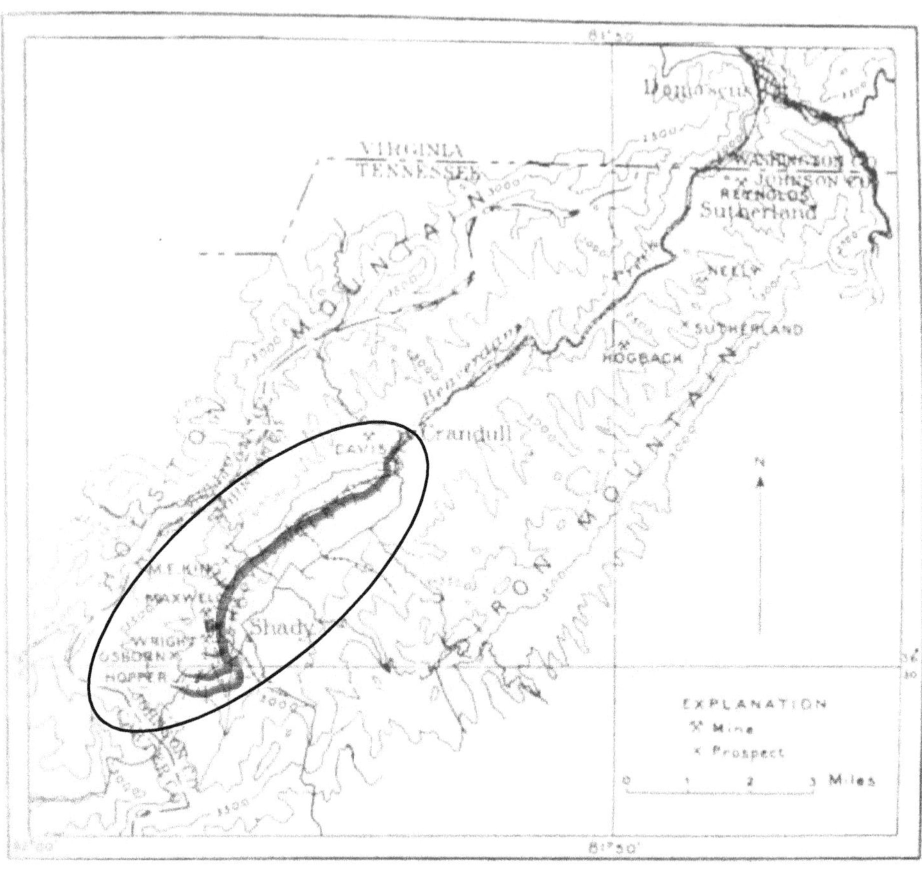


The segments operated by the BDRR/C&SVRy were:

Trackage rights over the Virginia–Carolina Railway – 1.386 miles

Beaver Dam Railroad – 8.500 miles

Crandull & Shady Valley Railway – 6.000 miles

Total (not including the approximately two miles of tracks serving ore developments) – 15.886 miles

# ABANDONMENT

Old Beaver Dam Railroad's roadbed through Backbone Rock Tunnel

Eventually, the timber areas became pretty well logged out, and the mining industry became unprofitable. With virtually nothing left to sustain the Beaver Dam Railroad's or the Crandull & Shady Valley Railway's trackages, these lines were abandoned in 1918.

The Empire Lumber and Mining Company stayed until 1909. By 1914, the Tennessee Lumber Manufacturing Company had cut all the trees of the size specified in its contract and moved out of Sutherland.

However, until well up in the late 1920s the Beaver Dam Railroad continued to exist in Virginia, using under lease the 1.386-mile branch of the Virginia–Carolina Railway to service the plant of the Smethport Extract Company. (The Smethport Extract Company's Damascus, Virginia plant was built in 1905 at the site of the Acme Bark Extract plant.)

Smethport Extract Company's
Damascus, Va. plant

Control of the Beaver Dam Railroad and the

Crandull & Shady Valley Railway passed into the hands of the Smethport Extract Company. On April 1, 1911, the Beaver Dam Railroad Company (of Va.), now owned by the Smethport Extract Company of Damascus, Virginia, formerly leased for 25 years to April 1, 1936, the Crandull & Shady Valley Railway at a monthly rental of $250. The lease, however, was surrendered on July 1, 1916.

The Beaver Dam Railroad Company (of Va.)'s rolling stock included 1 combination car owned by the Beaver Dam Railroad Company (of Va.), one combination car leased from the defunct Beaver Dam Railroad (of Tenn.), and the following leased from the Smethport Extract Company: locomotive – 1; freight cars (flat – 9; tank[15] – 23).

INCORPORATED UNDER THE LAWS OF
VIRGINIA

Number — Shares

Beaver Dam Railroad Company

CAPITAL STOCK $1000
Full paid and non-assessable

THIS CERTIFIES THAT

— Willie Hand — is the owner of — One — Shares of ONE HUNDRED DOLLARS each of the Capital Stock of the

transferable only on the Books of the Corporation in person or by Attorney upon surrender of this Certificate.

In Witness Whereof, the duly authorized officers of this Corporation have hereunto subscribed their names and caused the corporate Seal to be hereto affixed this 15th day of January A.D. 1926.

President

Treasurer

# TODAY

Backbone Rock Tunnel (Then)

Backbone Rock Tunnel (Now)

I'm sitting in a rocking chair on the porch of the Shady Valley Country Store drinking a Dr. Enuf soft drink. The store is located at the intersection of highways U.S.–421 and TN–133, about where the Bristol Road (today's highway U.S.–421) flag stop was. In my mind, I'm wearing bib overalls and waiting for the north-bound train to take me to Damascus, where I'm planning to hop on the north-bound Virginia–Carolina Railway train and ride all the way to Abingdon.

Besides hauling logs, lumber, ore, and extract bark, both the Beaver Dam Railroad's and the Crandull & Shady Valley Railway's mixed trains[16] also hauled a combined 2,000-plus passengers a year.

In my mind again, I hear the whistle of the approaching train and see off in the distance the smoke coming from the engine's stack. Quickly gulping down the last of my Dr. Enuf in one big swallow, I stand up from the rocker and pull from the back pocket of my overalls a red bandana, which I will use to flag down the train.

I'm shocked back to reality. The sound of the train's whistle was actually the sound of my son's Subaru's horn telling me that it's time to start our picture-taking trip up Tennessee's Highway 133 (the old Beaver Dam Railroad/Crandull & Shady Valley Railway roadbed). I look off in the distance. No smoke.

We pull into the Backbone Rock parking area. The Backbone Rock Tunnel seems to be the only reminder left that the Beaver Dam Railroad/Crandull & Shady Valley Railway ever existed. The tunnel is wider than it originally was, widened to accommodate two lanes of modern traffic, instead of steam locomotives on a single railroad track (I don't think the tunnel's height has changed; they apparently didn't have to chisel off more of the top of the tunnel so that modern cars and trucks could pass through, like the original builders had to do so that steam engines with tall smokestacks could pass through).

In the 1930s, the Civilian Conservation Corps (CCC) built stairs and a 0.4-mile-long trail that went over the top of the tunnel and across Backbone Rock.

A family who had been hiking the trail emerged at the trailhead at the edge of the parking area and began walking to the only other car. The father, when they got to where we were, showed us a video he had just taken with his cam-phone. It was a video of a great 'ol big rattlesnake slithering across the trail. After seeing the video, we decided not to hike the trail!

According to the GPS coordinates, the now-closed Neely Mine wasn't far away. I decided to go to it, even though I wasn't expecting much of the mine to be left. Opened in 1898 and closed in 1929, the Neely Mine, like Backbone Rock itself, is now a part of the Cherokee National Forest, the mine's pits filled to check erosion.

Closed Neely Mine

"It sure is spooky-looking around here," my wife said, as we were pulling out of the parking area.

"That's probably why they used to call most of the area we just drove through back there 'Haunted Hollow'," I said.

Thinking about the words "Haunted Hollow" brought to mind Benjamin H. Adams, Sr., who was mentioned earlier as having worked for both the Empire Lumber & Mining Company and the Tennessee Lumber Manufacturing Company. As a part of his experience, Mr. Adams is also quoted as saying:

[A few years later], *I went to work cutting timber for the Tennessee Lumber Manufacturing Company in the mountains near Backbone Rock. I remember one of my jobs was to get the logs out of "Hainted Hollow" to Alex Snyder, who ran the planing mill. A big fire broke out and everything I owned burned, except the clothes I was wearing. Many acres of young timber were destroyed. Homes burned. People loaded what possessions they could onto railroad flat cars and left the valley. Falling sparks started more fires on the flat cars; the people put them out, and finally reached a safe place.*

# NOTES

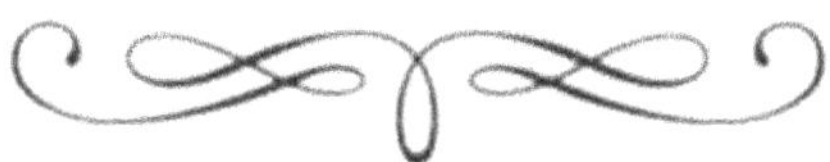

## NOTES

[1] Not all the mines and prospects shown on the map existed when the Beaver Dam Railroad existed.

[2] The difference between a prospect and a mine is this: a prospect is an area that *might* contain a commercially viable amount of a certain mineral/metal, but only a series of test holes can tell for sure; a mine is a place where a mineral/metal has been proven to exist in commercially viable amounts.

[3] Someone mentioned that her grandad was born in the area around what today is known as Crandull. She pointed out that it wasn't known as Crandull back then. Intrigued, I wanted to know how the area became known as Crandull. My theory: Almost always, when "Crandull" is someone's last name or the name of some community or town, "Crandull" is spelled with an "E" (CrandEll) or an "A" (CrandAll), not a "U". My theory is that since the lower part of Shady Valley is famous for its cranberry bogs, the "Cran" part of Crandull stands for "cranberry", The name of the president of the Empire Lumber and Mining Company was A. J. Dull, thus the "Dull" of "Crandull". Just a theory, so I might be completely off-base!

[4] Leather played a much bigger role in the past, than it does today. Back then, a wide variety of items: shoes, belts, hats, work aprons, and other articles of clothing, as well as horse saddles and other animal tack, just to mention a few things, were made of leather. Therefore, tanning was an important business. The extract that was used in the tanning process came from tree bark that was

high in its tannic acid or tannin content, such as the bark of hemlock, oak, and chestnut – trees that grew in abundance in the Shady Valley forests. In the early 1900s, the bark was bought by the extract company at a price of $6.00-$6.50 a cord (one cord of extract bark weights approximately 2,240 pounds). The market price of the liquid extracted from one cord (about 40 gallons) was $18.00.

[5] Although the Virginia–Carolina Railway's branch line to the Va./Tn. state line was 1.84 miles long, the trackage rights/rental agreement with the Beaver Dam Railroad was for 1.386 Miles of the branch, because that was the distance from the state line to the Acme Bark Extract plant.

[6] The engine was the Virginia–Carolina Railway's Engine #1, a 4-6-0 Baldwin. The numbers are the engine's Whyte notation, a classification method for steam locomotives by wheel arrangement. The notation in its basic form first lists the number of leading wheels (the V–C's Engine #1 had four leading wheels), then the number of driving wheels (the V–C's Engine #1 had six driving wheels), and finally the number of trailing wheels (the V–C's Engine #1 had zero trailing wheels), the numbers being separated by dashes. The word "Baldwin" meant that the engine was built by the Baldwin Locomotive Works of Philadelphia, Pennsylvania.

[7] A combination car is a railroad car containing two or more compartments used for different purposes (usually passengers, luggage, freight, and mail).

[8] The letter "T" in the Whyte notation means that a locomotive is a tank engine. A tank engine is a steam locomotive that carries its water supply in tanks mounted around its boiler, instead of in a

tender A tank engine might also carry its fuel supply on-board instead of in a tender.

[9] The Shay locomotive is a geared steam locomotive. Shay locomotives were especially suited for logging, mining and industrial operations and could operate successfully on steep or poor-quality track.

[10] A flag stop is a place where a train doesn't make regular stops but only stops if a passenger wants to get off or if someone outside flags the train down.

[11] The term "District" is used to designate a group of mines having a common geologic and geographic setting.

[12] A washer is used to remove clay and other impurities from the ore. One way of washing newly mined ore is by using a log washer, which is a slightly slanting trough in which revolves a thick shaft or log, carrying blades obliquely set to the axis. Material is fed in at the lower end, water at the upper. The blades slowly convey the lumps of material upward against the current, while any adhering clay is gradually disintegrated and floated out the lower end.

[13] Dry screening is the screening of solid materials of different sizes without the aid of water.

[14] An ore car has a capacity of about fifty tons.

[15] The tank cars were used to haul extract.

[16] A mixed train is a train that contains both passenger and freight cars.

# PHOTO & SOURCE CREDITS

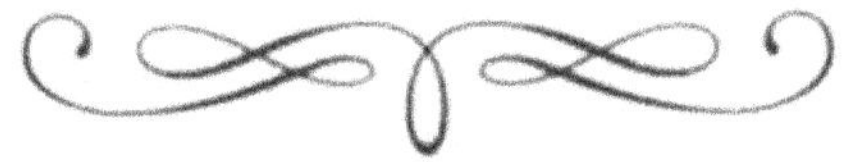

## PHOTO & SOURCE CREDITS

| | |
|---|---|
| Front Cover | Unknown |
| Back Cover | Courtesy of Jamey Eddy |
| Page 8 | Tennessee State Library & Archives |
| Page 11 | *The "Virginia Creeper": Remembering the Virginia–Carolina Railway* |
| Page 12 | Pocahontas County (WV) Historical Society |
| Page 14 | Courtesy of Jamey Eddy |
| Page 16 | Courtesy of Jamey Eddy |
| Page 17 | Unknown |
| Page 18 | Courtesy of Jamey Eddy |
| Page 20 | Unknown |
| Page 21 | Tennessee State Library & Archives |
| Page 22 (top) | *Resources of Tennessee* |
| Page 22 (bottom) | Tennessee State Library & Archives |
| Page 23 | Tennessee State Library & Archives |
| Page 24 | WWW.NewRiverNotes.com |
| Page 27 | G. N. Wertz |
| Page 30 | Tennessee State Library & Archives |
| Page 39 | Tennessee State Library & Archives |
| Page 46 | *Ghost Railroads of Tennessee* |
| Page 47 | WWW.NewRiverNotes.com |

**PHOTO & SOURCE CREDITS (CONTINED)**

| | |
|---|---|
| Page 48 | Washington County (VA) Public Library |
| Page 50 (top) | David McGuinn |
| Page 50 (bottom) | Unknown |
| Page 51 | David McGuinn |
| Page 53 | Doug McGuinn |

(Map on page V by Doug McGuinn)

www.ingramcontent.com/pod-product-compliance
Ingram Content Group UK Ltd.
Pitfield, Milton Keynes, MK11 3LW, UK
UKHW020137250726
13967UKWH00002B/719

9 781387 559916